KIN

HUGH DUNKERLEY

Cinnamon Press
:: small miracles from distinctive voices ::

Published by Cinnamon Press
Meirion House
Tanygrisiau
Blaenau Ffestiniog
Gwynedd, LL41 3SU
www.cinnamonpress.com

The right of Hugh Dunkerley to be identified as author of this work has been asserted by him in accordance with the Copyright, Designs and Patent Act, 1988. Copyright © 2019 Hugh Dunkerley.
ISBN: 978-1-78864-017-6

British Library Cataloguing in Publication Data. A CIP record for this book can be obtained from the British Library.

Designed and typeset in Palatino by Cinnamon Press. Printed in Poland.

Cover design by Adam Craig from original artwork 'Birth' by Diana Blok © Diana Blok, used with kind permission.

Cinnamon Press is represented in the UK by Inpress Ltd and in Wales by the Welsh Books Council.

Acknowledgements

I would like to thank the editors of the following magazines, anthologies and websites in which some of these poems first appeared: THE CLEARING, *The Creel* (Guillemot Press), *The Echo Room*, ECOZONA, *The Emma Press Anthology of Fatherhood*, *Irish Pages*, *Interdisciplinary Studies in Literature and Environment*, *The London Magazine*, *Underneath* (University of Canberra Poetry Prize Anthology), *The Blaze in My Father's Breath* (Winchester Poetry Festival Anthology 2018). I am grateful to The Arts Council of England for an award to aid the completion of this collection and to The University of Chichester for giving me time to take up the award. I am particularly grateful to the following for their support and feedback: Naomi Foyle, Robert Hamberger, Joanna Lowry, John McCullough, Dave Swann, Alison MacLeod, Stuart Pickford, Daniela Gerard, Stephanie Norgate and Dr Tim Rank. And, as always, to Bethan Roberts, just for being herself.

Biography

Hugh Dunkerley is a poet and ecocritic. He lives in Brighton with his wife and son and teaches at The University of Chichester, where he is Reader in Creative Writing and Contemporary Poetry. His lecture, 'Some Thoughts on Poetry and Fracking', won the 2016 INSPIRE/ASLE UKI Literature and Sustainability Public Lecture Award and was delivered at The Hay International Festival. His first collection, *Hare*, was published by Cinnamon Press in 2010.

Contents

Anatomy of a Breakdown

For Ted

Kin

We may all be netted together.

Charles Darwin

First Contact

I

Through a haze of ultrasound
we make you out, little amphibian

curled in your amniotic pool.
You're still a long way off,

still trying to conjure limbs,
kidneys, a central nervous system,

still wrestling with your DNA,
the fishtail that loops you

back into the Devonian.
On the monitor the nurse

picks out your infant heart
draining and filling with

new minted blood,
pulsing its tiny code of hope.

II

Almost unnoticed
you've slipped into our lives,

moored yourself to existence.
Even now you could slide

into non-being, re-enter
the ceaseless, inexorable

mill of the world
where the dead

and the yet-to-be-born
commune with glacial till,

dust from supernovas,
the sift of ten thousand summers.

III

Homunculus,
little cave dweller,

you're almost one of us,
a wordless prototype

waiting in the wings,
seeded with longings

and undaunted
after so long a journey;

a palimpsest of life's
infinite scribblings

but the only copy of you.

IV

With each passing month
you move through the constellations,

Aquarius, Gemini, Leo,
gathering mass and light,

your heavenly body arcing
across our night,

our waiting hands spread,
ready to catch you

in the net of love.

Quickening

When does being begin? I imagine you in the womb, a clutch of cells seething with division, a bud of life opening into spine, tubular heart, nascent limbs. They used to say the soul enters the body after forty days, hatched like a miraculous egg, though where it was before was anybody's guess. Now we're not so sure, talk of zygote, foetus, use the language of science, shy away from ascribing personhood to something we can never remember being. In a snowstorm of ultrasound, the nurse points to a shifting white patch, what could be an eel or the tail of a dragon for all I can tell. 'It's a boy,' she says, though whatever you are clearly isn't a person yet, a he or a she. It's the same way we talk about animals we haven't domesticated. 'It's a vixen,' we say, hearing that desperate child-like whine on a winter's night. The fox too moves beyond the pale of the human, male or female. And what about all the ones who never make it to birth? Were they ever there? What should we call that flicker of sentience, the moment when matter wakes up: *awareness, consciousness, soul*? Perhaps *being* is as close as we can get, more verb than noun.

Ode to a New Life Form

*TTA...TTG...*you stutter
out a new dialect
            unheard before
                    in the babble of
            chromosomes
    your DNA shaped
by computer
  and the human hand
            you will never touch
                    each microscopic
            mote of you
      parroting the same
cues until some
    slip or mischance
            changes
                    one of your offspring
            for the better,
    or worse,
  and the human
      hand loses
            control;
                    another turn in
      evolution's
  never-ending game
of Chinese
      Whispers,
            like the 3.8 billion
                    years of mishearings
        that led to this
    and this and this
hand, eye,
    consciousness
            these words writing
                themselves
        across a page.

*In May 2010, Craig Venter announced that he and his colleagues had synthesised a
microbe using chemically constructed blocks of DNA.*

Premature

I

The anaesthetist's still joking with you,
perspiration beading his thick moustache,
when I realise it's already started,

the rummaging in your womb,
your whole slack body shifting on the table,
the heads of the surgeon and his assistant

bobbing in and out of sight
beyond the green wall of cotton
they've rigged up to hide your lower half.

A sharp tug and it's all over it seems.
'Can you see him?' you ask,
panic in your voice, but I can only stand

legs swimming below me
as a long needling cry somehow
stitches itself into my brain.

II

What they give me to hold
seems too delicate to be exposed to air,
a small seed shucked early

from the fruit of your womb,
still matted with blood
and waxy with vernix,

a stunned survivor
slowly coming round,
tiny fists uncurling like ferns.

III

Under his dome, he's swaddled
in oversized baby clothes,
rigged up with an ECG,

apnoea monitor, the machines
chirping and whinnying,
his face below the blue bobble hat

shrivelled like an old man's in sleep.
When we take him out,
he cries at the light,

grasps your finger,
watches the semaphore of our smiles
from a far-off place

where words of comfort
can't reach him, where every breath
is a stumbling foothold.

Coming Home

You should still be in the womb -
a tender fish hooked too early -
as I carry you outside for the first time,
a cold westerly whipping around
the hospital's concrete canyons,
wrinkling your features.

In the waiting car we struggle
with the oversized child seat
and you begin to wail,
a tremulous, high-pitched call of distress,
your tiny limbs jerking with unaccustomed freedom.

I drive through rush hour traffic
as if the slightest bump could shatter you,
your mother's head pressed close to yours
in the rear-view mirror.

At home we will you to sleep,
pace up and down with your curled frame
clamped to our chests,
but nothing will comfort you,
nothing make up for the loss
of your first home in this world:

the ward with its fluorescent hum,
its constantly chattering monitors,
the small plastic tub where you lay swaddled
for three weeks in a womb of white
antiseptic smelling blankets.

Madonna and Child

Don't believe the lies:
Joseph was a randy little sod.
That's why we had to leave,
go back to Bethlehem
where he told his family
I was pregnant with the son of God.
Even they didn't believe him
and chucked us out, telling us
we could bunk down in the stable,
knowing what an animal he was.

But the boy, he was something else,
his miraculous, unblemished skin
pressed against mine,
his eyes watching my face
as if he could read my every mood.
I could even forgive Joseph,
shut away in his workshop,
drinking himself to pieces.
The boy was mine. No one
would ever take him from me.

Fist

You wouldn't sleep and nothing
we did made any difference
(you don't remember any of this,
you were a need in search of comfort)
and your mother was shushing you
in that old Ikea chair stained
with so many nights of feeding,
rocking you back and forth as you cried,
squirming from some pain
or bad dream you couldn't communicate.
And feeling utterly useless and exhausted
after so many sleepless nights,
I thumped the wall with my balled fist,
pushing all my rage through my arm,
and I heard the bone snap before I felt anything,
before my palm swelled to the size of a tennis ball,
before the burning pain made me double up
on the stairs outside, as I tried to keep silent,
so ashamed was I of what I'd just let myself do
and fearful too of what I'd let myself do
to that righteous friend who'd led me
through the world for so long, in whose
palm I'd cupped your small back and lifted you
when you were hauled, bloodied and bawling
from your mother's womb.

Evidence

Your handprints on the window
like those paint-blown silhouettes
deep in prehistoric caves.

In Vitro

Now there are five,
each one a life
on hold,

each singular
expression of DNA
locked tight

in a deep freeze.
After six years
they are still

seven days old:
she's stopped time
and doesn't know

what to do.
She'd carry them
close to her skin

if she could,
these sons
and daughters,

in cold rings
or on a necklace
of ice.

Night Drive

After three hours of road and noise
and lights strobing your sleeping face,
we've come to rest
on the corner of our street,

and with us the world:
the darkened houses,
the motionless cars, an enormous moon
looming over the trees.

Your mother's gone to open up
and apart from the car's ticking
and your breath coming and going
like a small tide over stones,

the only voices are the elms',
their leafy whisperings
moving like a conversation,
from tree to tree.

        Soon I'll carry you in,
your warm weight in my arms,
and you might stir,
open your eyes for a few seconds
and realise you're home.

Ant

Today you killed an ant,
        smearing it with your shoe
turning the word over in your mouth,
        testing its meaning,

although you struggle with the *t*
        as you bend down
to inspect the tiny wreckage
        of legs and feelers

splayed out on the garden path.
        I want to tell you about hurt,
explain how another creature,
        however small,

might know pain in the way you did
        when you slipped and fell
and came running to me,
        shocked by the bright red stain

forming on your palm. But you
        don't have those words yet
and anyway I remember how,
        much older than you,

I would happily and without thought
        tear a hook from the gasping mouth
of a mackerel, slam its head hard
        against the boat's side

until the whole thing went slack
        and it slid slowly down
to join its gunmetal brothers and sisters
        in the bucket on the deck.

The weight of all the world's ants
        is about that of the human race;
does the death of this one
        diminish the world in any way?

On the path other quick, black bodies
        are interrogating the flattened
thorax, the cock-eyed head
        but you're already busy

with the snail you've found,
        its tender horns reeling in
as you stroke the moist,
        disappearing animal.

Thrown

'Daddy, what's it like being you?' you ask, as if we could imagine any other state, could step outside our own being for a second and experience the profound shock of life as another. But then we would *be* someone else. The *you* that you are is the result of this becoming, no, it *is* this becoming. Being is always a mystery, even to ourselves. We are in it and of it. But to have being, to be thrown into this All, surely that's something. And to know you in this infinite flux of stars, mute stones and formless, timeless particles constantly making and unmaking everything, what are the chances of that? Let's ride this wave together, this arcing insubstantial moment.

The Refugee's Children

are dark-eyed and breathless,
all talking at once so what I hear is a babble of dialects,
the older boy's almost perfect English,
the twin girls with their heavy Iraqi accents,
the two-year-old squealing in any language
she cares to make up on the spot.
'Tea, tea,' their father says, disappearing into the kitchen
while the children swarm around me,
holding up pale dolls, drawings, stuffed animals,
pointing at the Arabic t.v. channel blaring in the corner
and laughing, always laughing
in this damp, half-forgotten seaside town
where their parents have brought them
so no one will try to kill them:
where the smallest girl dances
in the bare living room
with its peeling wallpaper
and hand-me-down sofa,
remembering nothing of war.

Crab Hunting at Llanidan

You're fascinated, watch as I lower
the line with its lump of snot-coloured
limpet into the white-wine water
swirling around the dock

until it settles on the bottom
and the line goes slack. Here,
among the swaying weeds
and the shifting grains of sand,

is what we've come for, though
you can only imagine it from pictures
and those tiny translucent
scuttlers we've seen on the beach

hurrying from rock to rock.
I pull in the line, the bait
bumping across the sand, stirring
up grains, small bronze fish

darting out of the weeds to tug
at the meat for a second and disappear.
Then, as the limpet begins to climb
the dock's side, all caverns

and seaworn stone, something
pulls hard on the line, a grasp
that will not let go, and I
haul up a small brown tank,

its feathery mouthparts moving,
its tiny eyes peering out from
under all that armour, one
freckled, overgrown claw

grimly hanging on to the shrivelled
bait, and you run, only stopping
to look back when I lower
the flailing monster into your child's

bucket where it struggles
to climb up the sheer plastic,
its helpless scrabblings rocking
the whole thing from side to side.

Twelve Weeks

You're lost now, my little rootling,
my deep-sea sailor,
my scaler of life's improbability.

We can't call you back
or make right again
the undone sum of your cells,

can't rewind to the first frame,
the one where the wrong sperm perhaps,
ardent and aflame,

buried itself in my egg's
pheromonal bliss.
This is all we'll ever know of you:

a rupture, a shedding,
a weightlessness, the space
where you might have been.

Her Hands

Once they were always hot,
red raw from squeezing out thick nappies
blood coursing through them
as she hoisted children, bags of shopping, boiling pans.
Worn skin left rashes
and she'd take off her wedding ring
to do the washing up, hanging it on a hook;
then, one morning, it was gone
but in those days there was no time for regret:
there were children to be fetched,
floors to be mopped, a husband to be fed.

Now her hands are cold;
she rubs the bruised, paper thin palms together
to little effect, wears gloves in summer.
The two of them have had enough,
are content to hold a pen,
some paper, make marks on an empty page,
say something of themselves;
though the memory of the moment
she crushed a glass deliberately
and without caring still lives
in the white weals on her left palm.

Ice Age Child

They left you
here, twelve
and a half

thousand years ago;
moved on,
following

the herds,
your yellowing
bones

curled under a cairn
of flints
this sharpened

elk bone
by your side
for the journey

between icefields,
through unknown
valleys

where you will
have to hunt
alone.

First Memory

There's no way back now
to the scent of cut grass
a whitewashed wall and a green door
the dark, oil-stained garage
my grandfather's Rover kennelled there
its huge back seat reeking of leather.

Pillboxes

Pissed in, scrawled with graffiti, their four
square blocks still squat at the bends of rivers,
by railways, or nestle into hillsides
camouflaged by coils of matted brambles.
As children, we clambered on their concrete
roofs, lobbed imaginary hand grenades
through gun slots, sprayed defenders
with mouthfuls of machine-gun spit.
Stepping inside, we'd enter a muggy
closeness, the semi-darkness freighted with
odd smells: sheep shit, the acrid scent of old
fires, tramp's bedding; wonder at the flaccid
sacks of rubber we found, something
milky clotted in their slack ends.

Rite

No longer able to bear the long drawn out
distress call of your absence,
they laid you gently on the back seat of the car,
wrapped in your Star Wars duvet,
then drove through an England
extravagant with summer - the chest-high
cow parsley wavering at the roadside,
the woods dense with cool greenery -
through traffic-jammed market towns
along the blur of a motorway,
until they arrived here, where wind
lifts choughs at the cliff's edge
and everything looks out on the empty spaces
of the glittering channel.
And here, perhaps, they said a final prayer
then strapped on their rucksacks—
the heavier one with your curled,
half-grown frame in it,
the other with toys,
your favourite plush rabbit, a plastic tractor –
and they walked into air.

Ammonite

Striated with quartz, it's two feet across and must weigh quarter of a ton. You stare through the gift shop window in this small French town, fascinated by the polished bulk, the sheer stoniness of something that once floated in water. 'Is it still alive?' you ask and I try to explain what a fossil is, how this isn't even the creature itself but its echo in rock reaching us sixty-five million years late, how the houses around us are built from the bodies of numberless sea creatures. For a moment the cafés, the boutiques with their bright clothes shipped in from India, Bangladesh, China, the shifting flows of tourists, seem a trick of the light, something conjured by the heat. The others have all gone: Habilis, Erectus, Heidelbergensis, Floresiensis, Neanderthal; sifted in the dust of the millennia; all that's left are a few bones, some tools, scattered grave goods. What are seven and half thousand generations but a blink of evolution's eye? And yet, here we are, two waking moments *alive alive O,* standing upright on the bed of an ancient sea.

The Red Telephone

I remember buying a telephone,
red, a seventies replica,
on the day your mother told me she was pregnant;
standing in the shop in Bristol
and wondering, selfishly, what would become of my life.

You were just an idea,
hardly more than a niggle of cells
fructifying in the womb,
nothing to show for yourself except
a daily nausea in your mother's stomach.

No part of you even knew it existed
and yet the wet Christmas streets
glittering in the four pm dusk,
the steamy-windowed cafés

seemed altered somehow;
even the red telephone
hanging stupidly from my hand
was loud with expectation.

The Eel

after Montale

Eel, siren of cold oceans,
quitting the Baltic for our seas,
our estuaries, our rivers,
coming up from the deeps,
nosing under the downstream surge
from tributary to tributary,
stream to stream,
wanting to get back inside,
to get to the heart of rock,
infiltrating rills of mud, until one day
light glancing off chestnuts
ignites her fuse in stagnant puddles,
in ravines cascading
from Apennine flanks to the Romagna;
eel, torch, whip,
arrow of Love on earth,
only our gullies,
our parched alpine streams
lead back
to the paradise of insemination;
green soul seeking life
where there is only drought and desolation,
the scintilla that says
everything begins again
when all seems burnt through,
reduced to a buried stump;
that quick iridescence,
refracted now in your unclouded eyes;
sons of man, immersed in your mud,
can you not see she is your sister?

The Chase

It's beautiful, this chase across the desert,
sand kicking up in the dying light,
bright with the sun's momentary glance,
the loping, athletic lions moving in slo-mo,

the giraffe galloping into shot,
disappearing behind a solitary tree,
then emerging again, the lions closer now.
Up ahead, Attenborough tells us breathlessly,

the pride's leader waits, nervy in the scrub,
flings herself headlong at the giraffe,
bounces off to hit the ground,
hooves trampling her, but still she gets up,

shakes her tawny pelt, watches
the dwindling prey disappear over a hill,
the music slowing, though we've hardly
been aware of the crescendoing chords,

so used are we to having our sympathies tugged,
to the thrill of the chase.
And I want to believe it's true,
that the plains are endless, the herds

inexhaustible, the only humans
bit players from the Pleistocene.
In our sitting rooms, on our phones,
at thirty-thousand feet, we dream the world without us.

Widow

Nothing has prepared her for this,
the capsizing house, the relentless days,
the television moaning in the background.

The hours panic, each one battering
its stall, worse than the last,
the armchair, the unpaid bills,

the exhausted sofa all closing in.
Even the garden's gone guerrilla:
roses he pruned hard every winter

plague the glass with their thorns;
ivy fingers the back-bedroom window
while inside her son's childhood

clings on in *The Illustrated Iliad,*
The Muppet Show, the dented Matchbox
cars lining the dusty shelves.

In the double bedroom, the mattress sags,
still remembering his weight,
the familiar tideline of sweat,

the sprawl of his long restless limbs;
every night she tries to fill it,
sleeplessness gnawing her to the bone.

Song for the Song of the Common Starling

For Don McKay

thoughts
        around a wild idea
they condense, all squealing
their hoarse electronica,
their barely contained epilepsy

clot the top of an elm

then the insane skull-tapping,
the emphysemic wheezing,
the saucy *cor blimey*
pipsqueaking whistles,

as if the tree has burst
into a half-cocked song

or is it a conversation—
impossible to know what's going on
in that fevered bird-brain

and suddenly they're gone,
branches still rebounding,
the air beaten and stirred in their wake.

Exile

In the end, little of what he said made any sense.
We followed him blindly, abandoning
our boats, our families, our ragged tents,
becoming outcast like him, almost starving
when villages shut their doors on us.
It all seemed so hopeless, scratching
about out there in the desert, at a loss.
Sometimes he just seemed to be listening,
crouched for hours, rocking on his heels,
muttering what could have been a prayer.
He spoke in riddles; mustard seeds, pearls,
'Split the wood, look for me. I am there.'
Just once he brushed my forehead with a kiss.
'The Kingdom,' he whispered, 'it's as close as this.'

Aphasic

The blood clot stalled
and the synapses died;
language faltered,
the breath-blown vowels,
the precise consonants
stuttering to a halt.

For those last months
your mouth became a farmyard
of gurgles, sheep calls,
swinish grunts and strangled squeals,
your frustration in that banging arm
you summoned your wife with;

you who'd loved words,
the dry rustle of abstractions,
the barked riddle,
meaning shearing off
like a cornice
in the high, pure air.

Nuclear Dreams

I

Scanning the headlines, all I could make out
were *Cruise* and *Reagan*;
the Italians were swarming the newsstands,
the occasional words 'Guerra', 'Bomba'
rising above a stream of panicky syllables.
Would I die, incinerated
in this bright city on the Adriatic,
far from any family or friends,
or worse, survive
to pick amongst the rubble,
puking with radiation while Britain
smouldered, a heap of ashes?
'Gaddafi, Gaddafi,' one man was shouting.
'Ora ci ucciderà.' I looked again at the headlines.
Tripoli I read, relieved that this time
it was someone else's war.

II

We were cubbed in fear,
coming just after The Cuban Missile Crisis
and before China's first bomb,
wondering about contrails,
the submarines with their world-ending cargoes
nosing down the Clyde.
Our parents had no answers,
as if they'd grown immune, or stopped
noticing it could happen at any moment.
The shrieking of nothing is killing,
just pictures of Jap girls in synthesis, Bowie sang
as we watched the first missiles arrive at Greenham
and Korean Airlines 007 plunged into the sea.

III

On the news we saw the burning reactor,
helicopters flailing like dying insects
in the updraft. It was all grainy sepia,
as if radiation had infested the film;
isotopes were falling on Vienna, Warsaw,
coating the surgical whiteness of the alps.
The sheets on the line, the spring-green grass,
took on a new meaning. Rain felt like electricity,
each bright drop whispering
Caesium, Barium,
strange half-remembered words
from the chemistry lab at school,
the huge Periodic table glowing on the wall.

Referendum

On the night of the vote
thunder boomed across the city,
its echoes crumbling into the distance.

I slept badly, woken
by livid flashes of light,
nagging dreams and premonitions.

We don't believe in portents anymore
but maybe, just this once,
the lie was so enormous

it shook the old gods from their slumber.

Anatomy of a Breakdown

Dread

Somehow the present is never enough,
the scoured sky,
the green tree of now
translucent with seeing.

Instead the racketing mind
must keep putting its eye to that keyhole
which it imagines is the future
and which is always dark with becoming.

Telescopic

Suddenly the moon came closer,
its pockmarked monochrome bulging
out of darkness, half of it still in night.
He thought of boiling on that desert,
of radiation and airlessness.
'Look how it's moving,' his brother said,
taking a turn at the eyepiece.
And when he looked again
he could see the whole thing had shifted.
'It just proves there's a God, all that order.'
But all he could see were billions of tons
bowling, untethered, through nothingness.

Losing it in the Natural History Museum

It comes down to this

> *ninety-nine point nine per cent*

the bones of the dead

> *of species*

are everywhere

> *that ever lived*

juggled into airy jigsaws

> *are gone*

and us looking at them

> *entailing*

trying to forget what we are

> *Divergence of Character*

will become

> *and the Extinction*

who will

> *of less improved forms*

remember

> *Please do not dispose of*

us?

> *No Exit.*

Prayer

Our father, who art in hiding,
harrowed be thy name,
thy kingdom gone, thy will undone
on earth as it is.
Give us this day our daily bloodshed
and forgive us our terrors
as we would forgive the terrors of others.
Lead us not into despair
but deliver us from belief
for thine is the crisis, the powerlessness
and the absence
for ever and ever
amen.

Carapace

It thickens, requires almost daily effort now
to keep airways open, to allow
any light to penetrate its darkening cells.

In Praise

O Escitalopram,
intercessor in the intrasynaptic
levels of blessed serotonin,
you block the re-uptake
of the neurotransmitter
in the presynaptic neuron
and thus bring about
the stabilisation of mood,
a benison for which we give veneration.

Thanks be to thee.

O Zopiclone,
we magnify thy bounty,
a cyclopyrrolone
which with zeal and devotion
increases the normal transmission
of the neurotransmitter
gamma-Aminobutyric acid
causing depression and tranquilisation
of the central nervous system
and lets us sleep.

Thanks be to thee.

O Diazepam
for the propitiation of the gods of panic,
you act via micromolar bonding sites
and thus increase the inhibitory processes
in the bewildered cerebral cortex.
We extol thee for the inhibition
of the polygraphic pathways
of the spinal cord.

Thanks be to thee.

Sanctuary

When the blade misses the vein,
when the pills fail to work,
when the noose breaks,
when the exhaust hose is jerked
loose at the last moment;

when you curl like a foetus
in a sweat-soaked bed,
when you're juddering with panic,
when you hurl your head
against the bedroom wall;

when the next moment seems
impossible to bear,
when every sinew's raddled
with fear, when you stare
through your children.

When you've had your fill,
they bring you here,
put a tiny orange pill
like God's own holy wafer
on your tongue
and you sleep.

Air Show

They're both in the corridor and duck instinctively
as the air splits and a roar booms across the sky
leaving trees, buildings, clouds shaking in its wake.

Next time they're quicker, rush to the office window,
see a swarm of small red jets streaking through the cloudscape,
red, white and blue streaming out behind them.

Glimpsed for a few seconds, the planes are gone,
the horizon already too small, their speed eating up the miles
then spitting them out with unimaginable haste.

'Fantastic,' she says, 'it must be better than sex,
travelling that fast,' while he thinks of that village
in Helmand, roof timbers still smouldering,

the blank-eyed children by the roadside,
of crouching with nowhere to hide
under that torment of sound.

Self-Portrait as a Francis Bacon

You painted with a scalpel,
            each canvas a wound
                        excavated by pain,
the body always something

flayed and suffering,
            the human mouth opened
                        again and again
in a howl of agony or despair,

canines bared. The only dog
            is circling, savage with fear,
                        its blackened flesh
looking as if it's been incinerated.

The first time I saw your pictures
            I remember stumbling clear
                        of the gallery,
the screaming popes, eviscerated lovers,

faces with half their skin scraped off
            still ringing in my mind.
                        I stepped into the din
of a London afternoon,

the lights just coming on,
            streets glittering,
                        the faces passing me
taut with anguish,

eyes blind with exhaustion,
            nerves, sinews, tendons
                        all rippling beneath
pale November skin.

*

Stop, wait. Rewind.
        Was that really the way it happened?
         Didn't I in fact enjoy
something of your revulsion,

the way you kicked traditional painting
        in the teeth, immersed yourself
         in horror?
I was nineteen, nibbling

at the fringes of Sartre and Camus,
        unsure of what I needed
         but needing it, whatever it was,
to be clean and true.

'To know the scheme of things,
        to clear my cluttered mind
         of all the junk built up over time,'
I wrote, thinking I could throw over the past,

make it all new. The gallery was intimate,
        sexual, scented with paint
         and the bodies of the
people moving through it.

I was alone in London.
        I could be anyone I chose.
         'Man is a blank slate'
you wrote.

I wanted to believe you,
        wanted to feel something
         of your great pain,
wanted to feel something.

Excision

Something had swelled
        and fattened,
a small translucent bead
        on your chest,

and was swelling still;
        'A rodent ulcer,'
the tall dermatologist said,
        as if giving it

that nomination
        could consign it
to things that are bad,
        unwanted,

diseased, yet it was a part
        of you,
cells blindly going about
        their business,

following the garbled
        orders
of sun-damaged DNA.
        Easy enough to fix—

a ten-minute procedure
        as I stood
holding your hand,
        unable to look

at the bright scalpel
        slicing
through skin, the blood spring
        opening.

        *

'At our age it's like
        the flu,'
the nurse said
        as Naomi dressed

after her biopsy,
        a bolus of cells
thickening in her breast.
        Cancer,

from the Greek
        Karkinos,
the swollen veins like the legs
        of a crab:

something of its tenacity,
        hunkering
down under attack,
        unmoved

by appeals; its creaturely
        ambition;
the way it has to be
        rooted out.

Creosote

Back gardens; the endless summers
of the seventies when it seemed to be light
until midnight and the lawn burned down

to a few pale roots in the dust.
Someone was always creosoting,
slapping the Coca-Cola coloured liquid

onto a fence or a shed,
the tarry petroleum tang
hanging in the hot air.

If you got close enough and breathed hard
your head would spin
and the world tip for a few seconds

before the garden found its feet again.
One summer, twelve, I was covering a fence,
the stuff running down my arms,

soaking into the too-big gloves
I'd been given for the job.
This is what men do, I remember thinking,

the slippy brush in my hand,
my nostrils burning,
and the two girls in the next garden,

—the ones who only a year before
had boy's bodies —
peeping over their own gravy-brown fence.

'Sex maniac,' they kept shouting,
then ducked down and though the words
were adult and unfamiliar,

I knew they had something to do
with the weightless feeling in my groin
as I imagined their small breasts

pressed against the rough, hairy wood,
whatever it was between their legs
slippery and wet in the heat.

Submarine Graveyard

From the road you see them,
blunt hulks hemmed in now
by flaking barges,

redundant landing craft,
the ground that has grown
around them a pelt

of rosebay willowherb
and rutted, oil-stained grass.
De-fanged, stripped

of their deadly burden,
they kilter at a lean.
Anything of value's been plundered,

conning towers gutted,
wiring pulled out
like so much spaghetti,

decks ripped off and trucked away.
Only the dense, immovable
hulls remain,

subsiding slowly into mud,
the land healing over them,
a new peninsula inching

into the bay;
though their kin
still plough the seas

or lurk unseen,
their payloads
simmering with readiness.

Nightmare Ground

For Keith Douglas

Somewhere near here you died,
killed instantly when a mortar round
exploded in the air above you

its furious shrapnel driving
itself into your brain with such efficiency
no entry wound could be found.

You were buried by a hedge,
with a few quick words from the padre,
before your unit moved on.

In two years of war
you'd seen hundreds dead:
burnt abandoned corpses

mummified in the desert sun,
the newly killed looking
as if they'd just fallen asleep,

your own gunner shredded
in the tank beside you,
'the turret in a flurry of blood'.

On leave in Tel Aviv, Cairo,
laid up in El Ballah General Hospital,
you began to forge lines

tempered by the steely glare of war,
each bullet-like poem
a fresh skirmish,

almost an epitaph,
a new language whose accents
we're still trying to master.

(Normandy, 2017)

In the Ermita San Miguel

the saint is standing over Satan,
wings outstretched, a spear pinioning
the scarlet, goat-horned figure to the ground.
The saint's face is impassive,
as if he's used to this sort of thing
but Satan's eyes are locked on Miguel's,
his mouth open, a long phallic tongue yearning;
pendulous breasts hang from his chest,
his torso disappearing into scales
and a flickering double tail.
Who wouldn't look at him,
the centre of this altarpiece,
raw with animality
while all around the saints
stare, blank-eyed, from their niches?

Return

After the vast body of North America,
the Atlantic's four-hour absence,
these islands are like a child's drawing,
the patchwork fields,
the land worked over and over.

As the plane banks,
I hold the South East
in my eye: the bulge of Kent,
a white cliff somewhere near Hastings,
and in the distance, the glistening Thames.

How small it is, this archipelago
nudging Europe's hip,
one foot in the Channel,
its granite head swimming with memories
of the Norse,

Ireland like a deflated football
kicked again and again
for the sheer hell of it.
Dig anywhere
and you'll find something

human: musket, handaxe,
fibre-optic cable, the numberless
bones of the dead. London
comes up to meet us
sunlight seething off a window,

its lost rivers—the Fleet,
the Tyburn, the Effra -
its plague pits and bombsites,
buried now under rearing towers,
steel carapaces, hives of glass.

Song

In All Saints on the corner of The Drive
                    and Eaton Road
my father strains to hear the tenor,
as he tells us the next song
by Ivor Gurney was written in the trenches
one hundred years ago.

'I think I need a hearing aid,' my father whispers,
asking me to repeat the tenor's words

but then the first chords of the piano
rise, limpid in the placeless air
and the tenor climbs his way up
the ascending moments of a song
which is both now and the moment
when it arrived in Gurney's head
and all is clear.

Ode to Ted

My boy, my wee one,
　　　my beansprout sprouting,
my live wire leaping,
　　　my conjurer conjuring words from thin air.

My little man, my buckaroo,
　　　my reeling laugher, my show-stealing
larger-than-life *what shall we do?*
　　　wrecker of rooms.

My simmering pot, my gene-genie
　　　my up-with-the-dawn
havoc wreaker, my brawling bawler,
　　　my loudspeaker.

My joker, my bamboozler,
　　　my natter-jack nattering, my stickler
my struggler, my *can I sit on your head?*
　　　dad mugger.

My new life, my one and only
　　　never-to-be-repeated leaping lord,
my priceless hoard,
　　　my darling, my son.